THIS BOOK BELONGS TO:

_____

This book is for my littlest barista, Evan.
You are kind, strong, funny, and the best coffee buddy a
mother could ever ask for.

Copyright © 2021 Melissa Cummings

Published by Cummings Press Ltd.
Glassboro, NJ

Printed in USA
ISBN 978-1-7376164-1-2
Library of Congress Control Number: 2021915131

Good morning, friend! Welcome to my street,
where my family owns a cafe with sweet pâtisseries.*
We live on the second floor, and just below,
is our cozy cafe where the coffee flows.

*pâtisseries- French pastries

Each morning at dawn, Grandma bakes and prepares
delicious and beautiful chocolate eclairs
from a recipe used for generations,
made for seventy years at this location.

I wrap pastries in parchment to put on display
to sell to our customers to brighten their day.

We serve hot coffee and cold coffee, too.

Grinding the beans is such fun to do!

My mama lifts me and holds me up high
as I write the drink of the day on our sign.
On our menu, we have a new cup size called "tista",
inspired by me, the Littlest Barista.
It measures six ounces, the perfect amount
for kids my age who are strolling about.

TRY OUR
NEWEST
SIZE
TISTA 6 OZ

TIPS

So when they come in for a quick, little sip,
they can pick the right size for their hot chocolate.

We unlock the door, put on our aprons,

and open the shop to our neighborhood patrons.

I grab my step stool and place it behind the counter,

then stand next to my papa who couldn't be prouder.

The first customer today is a regular here;
she visits our shop every day of the year.
"Good morning, Miss May," I smile and say.
"What can we get started for you today?"

HONEY

"A large coffee would be an absolute dream,
with a cube of sugar and a side of sweet cream."

Mr. Thomas stops by to order his usual,
an espresso with whipped cream, so visually beautiful.

The grinder whirls with beans that have loads of flavor
giving our customers lots to see, smell, and savor.

Papa dumps the ground beans into the press;
I push down the tamper for it to compress.

I reach for the button to start up the machine,
and out of the top bellows warm clouds of steam.
It bubbles and hums; what a wonderful sound!
I ready the cup as the hot liquid flows down.

Together we hand our customers their cups
and look through the line to see who's next up.
Officer Flank orders a sweet puff pastry,
which is nothing less than deliciously tasty.

Papa helps by holding the bag open wide;
I grab the tongs and place the pastry inside.

The cafe gets busy; I start rushing around
and forget the hot cup that I just put down.
Over it spills! Oh, it makes such a mess!
Now poor Mr. DuMont is coffee-less.

"It's OK to slow down, son, and just take your time.
I'm happy to wait. You're doing quite fine!"

I take a deep breath and count to ten,
then gather the courage to try it again.

Mama hands me a cup; Papa stands by my side as I carefully pour the hot beverage inside.

With the steamed milk, I make a special desig to thank him for being patient and kind.

"I'll see you tomorrow- same place, same time."
With a smile and a wave, Mr. DuMont says
goodbye.

Before I know it, the clock strikes one,

and Mama, Papa, and I are all done.

I wipe down the counter, tables, and chairs.

Then I take for myself the remaining eclair.

Another lovely day seeing people from town,
serving the finest coffee and pastries around.
We say thank you to our customers near and far,
but for now, friend, I will say au revoir*.

*au revoir- good-bye
*la fin- the end

Made in the USA
Middletown, DE
02 August 2023